HERE'S LOOKIN' AT LIZZIE

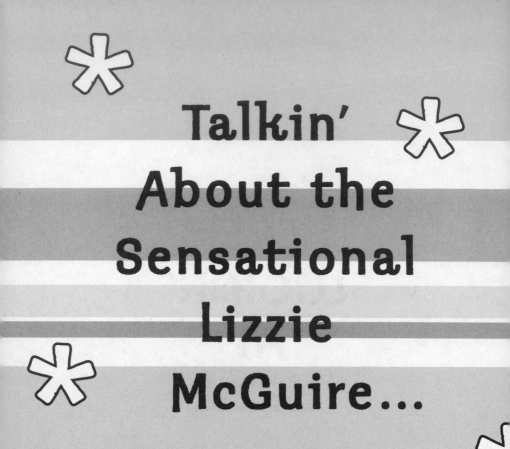

Talkin' About the Sensational Lizzie McGuire...

HERE'S LOOKiN' AT LizziE

Guen Sublette

St. Martin's Griffin ⪰ New York

www.stmartins.com

Book design by Nick Wunder

ISBN 0-312-32670-X

First Edition: August 2003

10 9 8 7 6 5 4 3 2 1

To my darling pre-tweens,

Jonah William Sublette
and
Sandra Jean Sublette

Contents

Acknowledgments

A huge thank-you goes out to all the young people across the country who made this book possible with their invaluable, creative insight and candor. Gratitude is also in profuse order for the teachers and administrators who helped muster input from their "troops" of preteen "tweens": Kathy Namura, Mike Cawthra, Nancy Stephens, Tim Moore, Melissa Sublette, and Julie Williams. And profound appreciation to all my friends and family who put up with my temporary departure from the regular responsibilities of mom-dom to immerse myself in the all-consuming, wonderful yet turbulent world of tweens.

introduction

There's no doubt that the long-locked, freckle-nosed Lizzie McGuire is a sensation. Who *doesn't* love a long-legged girl who can stumble and fall ridiculously in front of her entire junior high school and still manage to recover and come across as adorable—downy hazel-brown eyes blinking innocently—not to mention the ability to take the stage and sing out in a sultry voice like a real pop star?

Enamored fans from across the nation yearn to be like Lizzie—to dazzlingly prevail despite the adolescent angst that comes with having legs that grow faster than a mind can think, or they just wish they could have a best buddy like her. No matter the situation, Lizzie imparts charm and humor thanks in large part to her animated alter ego—the inner cartoon self who can scream out her innermost feelings even when the situation warrants little more than a humble outward smile.

Perhaps the most appealing feature about "Toon Lizzie," as the inner cartoon self has been called, is the fact that she's timeless: Her spirited voice continues to ring out true to "tweens" everywhere, no matter what path Lizzie, or the actress who plays her character on the TV show and in the movie (Hilary Duff), takes.

Indeed, what every girl needs isn't a raspy voice, perfect manicure, and curlicue swinging locks of beautiful blond hair, but an alter ego the likes of Lizzie's. (Boys could surely use one, too!) And here we give readers that opportunity, with an inside look at how tweens across the country really feel about Lizzie. We've also included a reflection section called "Your Imaginary Friend" at the end of each chapter that will let you look at your own feelings, as well as find some tips on how to deal with those feelings.

Who do you see in your reflection? And what words do you hear? Listen closely and you may find that your own alter-ego imaginary friend, like Lizzie's, is not only a timeless but also a very wise and cherished pal.

HERE'S LOOKIN' AT LIZZIE

1 ✳

Friends—Who Needs 'Em Anyway?

What a cutie: In *The Lizzie McGuire Movie*, Lizzie meets a new friend, Paolo, who proves irresistible, what with his dimpled olive complexion, smooth Italian accent, "great hair," and shiny red motor scooter. In fact, he's everything Lizzie's longtime, messy-haired pal Gordo *isn't*. He's also quite different from classmate Ethan, who worries more about shreddin' the wheels of his skateboard on Roman cobblestones than finding adventure and romance under the twinkling nighttime lights of an ancient *Città Eterna*. *Duh,* who wouldn't trade a dreary old pal and juvenile skateboard wheels for a crazy chance on a speedy moped?

As Lizzie learns, however, a crazy chance doesn't always lead to the outcome you'd expect. For one, it brings longtime snobbish rival Kate to her side as an unexpectedly supportive chum. Go figure: Add one little "r" to the word *fiend,* and you've got a "friend"!

What's more, good old boy-pal Gordo turns out to be one of the best friends Lizzie could ever hope for. For some, having a boy who's just a friend (rather than a romantic diversion like Paolo) can be a bit tricky. Like, what should you talk about? Take a tip from Gordo and try telling some old half-forgotten joke about the king of Norway. (OK, so maybe that's *not* the best advice after all. But at least it's a good way to stall for time if you need it!)

We asked girls and boys from across the country what they've learned from watching Lizzie, what it takes to be a real friend, and how to keep your old friends. Read on for some unexpected insights on friendship!

KiDS' COMMENTS:

Katilyn, 13

One thing you might learn from watching Lizzie is that you shouldn't judge someone by what they look like but how nice they are to you and your friends. I hope that I can trust my friends and my family. It's important to always talk to them and never be mean or talk about them behind their backs. How you can tell that someone is a friend is by being nice to them and they are nice back to you. That's how you know whether someone is a real friend.

I was not surprised that Lizzie became better friends with Kate in the movie because they had always been friends, but when they are with their separate friends they hate each other. I think that it made the movie more interesting.

Brigid, 12

Friends are people you can trust. You can keep your old friends by staying loyal. You can tell someone is a good friend when they stay loyal, like Gordo is to Lizzie in the movie as well as on the TV show.

I was, but I sort of wasn't, surprised that Lizzie and Kate became better friends at the end of the movie because Kate was mean most of the time, but she and Lizzie used to be BFs (see "Speaking of Which" section at end of book for a glossary of tween terms such as this one).

Nicole P., 10

I can trust my friends especially if they are faithful. I can keep my old friends by not fighting or being mean to them. You can tell by their attitude who's a friend.

I think it was good that Lizzie and Kate became better friends in the movie because Lizzie and Kate always argue. You should never fight with friends.

Bailey, 11

I pick a lot of the same types of friends as Lizzie—like Miranda and Gordo. At my age it's not a problem having a friend who's a boy. Maybe when I get older it will be different.

❧   ❧   ❧

Being just friends with someone of the opposite sex can sometimes get a bit complicated—especially as you get older. "I don't understand girls," says Lizzie's little brother, Matt. Even Lizzie sometimes wonders about the just friends relationship she has with pal Gordo. "Why do I feel all flushed and light-headed?" she wonders, in one TV episode when Kate tells her that Gordo has a crush on her. In another episode, Lizzie tries to change herself to become someone Ethan likes as more than "just a friend." In the end, Lizzie learns that her true pals—no matter what their sex—are the people who trust and care for her.

Michael, 9

Sometimes all the characters in the TV show are enemies. Once they had a race and at the end, near the finish line, Lizzie said sorry first to everyone, then they all said sorry back and they all crossed the finish line together. I liked it because they didn't have their usual friends as partners— Gordo was with Kate, Miranda was with Larry, and Lizzie was with Ethan. It taught me to say sorry first when you get in a fight. If it doesn't work, just walk away.

Kameron, 11

I think Kate (deep, deep down) is a nice person, but she's afraid to show it.

I learned from the movie that a *real* friend will sacrifice just about *anything*.

As a boy, I know what it's like to have friends who are girls because *most* of my friends *are* girls. It's the same as having a friend who's a boy.

Mary, 10

If you like someone and you ignore your friend, they get their feelings hurt. You can trust someone who's never told one of your secrets. You can keep your old friends by not getting into fights and get each other's phone number or new phone number if they move.

You can tell if someone's a good friend by asking their other friends what they think about them or know about them.

I think it's a good thing that Lizzie and Kate became better friends in the movie because now they can get to know more about each other.

Dylan, 8

You know someone's a good friend if you play with them every day. If they are mean to you and say, "Shut up," and, "Duh," they're not usually my friend.

If you ask a boy to help you with something and he does it, you know he is your friend, like Gordo is to Lizzie.

Morgen, 11

You can have more than one best friend. I can trust all of my friends. I can tell if someone is a good friend because they don't make you choose who your friends are.

* * *

In one TV episode, Lizzie becomes friends with the rebellious, "tormenter extraordinaire" Angel and ditches her old pals Gordo and

Miranda in exchange for an exciting new friendship and style that includes tattoos, nose rings, and a defiant attitude. When she takes it too far, Gordo and Miranda finally pull her aside and tell Lizzie she needs to stop—that she shouldn't act like someone she's not. Luckily for Lizzie, she listens to her old friends. Sometimes your old friends can help you remember who you really are.

Elise, 12
Sticking together (like Lizzie and her friends do) is very important because you'll have your friends no matter what, even if you're mad at them.

Laura, 10
You can trust people as friends if they don't speak badly about anyone.

Ashley, 11
Lizzie and Kate are such different people, so I was surprised when they became better friends.

Courtney, 12
It is good to make lots of new friends, but it is great to have a couple of good friends that you can really trust.

❋ ❋ ❋

Everyone who watches Lizzie on TV probably wishes they had a couple of good pals like Gordo and Miranda. They're trustworthy, caring, supportive, and—for the most part—consistent, unlike Kate, who shows friendship for fleeting moments, then quickly snaps back to her snobbish, sarcastic self. After a short-lived sweetness and appreciation for something Lizzie does to help her, for example, Kate is quick to quip, "Glad that's behind us!" and then returns with a flip of the hair to her original, conceited state.

Paulina, 11

I knew Kate and Lizzie would be friends again because they were very good friends when they were little, and once you have a good friend, you never lose them.

Sy, 12

You can trust a person if they don't make fun of you.

Maybe I would like to have Lizzie as a friend. As a boy, you're just friends with girls and not really, really good friends.

❈ ❈ ❈

"I guess I'm just the guy you say 'Hi' to in the hallway—not the guy you should go out with," laments Gordo in one TV episode. Trying to distinguish between just friends and more than friends can indeed be tricky!

Sarah, 11

You can keep old friends and make new ones. You can trust people who care about you. You keep your old friends by not ignoring them when you find new ones. If someone is your friend, they care about you and they won't just ditch you!

Karyssa, 12

You should always stay loyal to your friends. When you make new friends, you shouldn't forget about your old friends. A way to keep the old friends is to remember all the good times you had with them.

I think you can tell good friends from bad friends because good friends accept you as who you are and don't try to change you to "be cool."

I was surprised that Lizzie became better friends with Kate in the movie because Kate is usually mean to her. I think it's good that they became friends because they used to be such good friends, and it was sad when they weren't friends anymore.

Emilie, 9

No matter what happens you should always keep your friends. I can trust all four of my other friends. I just always keep my old friends. If someone's a good friend, they can trust you and keep secrets.

It was cool that Kate and Lizzie became friends at the end of the movie because in only two of the episodes was Kate being nice to Lizzie. I also think that they should be friends.

Cody, 12

You should get to know someone before you become friends with them. I can trust my best buddy, Danielle. I keep my old friends by calling them on the phone or writing them letters. I can tell if someone's a good friend if they are caring, nice, honest, and don't tell other people your secrets.

I think it was a very good thing that Lizzie became better friends with Kate at the end of the movie.

Merissa, 10
It's so weird that Kate is so mean.

Kaley, 11
You can't trust too many people when you first get to know them, but after you get to know them, you might feel like you can trust them. After you make a friend, you don't want to lose him/her. One way to keep a friend is to not lose interest in them. Don't forget to include them in your activities.

It's hard to not like someone, and it's better to have friends than enemies.

Taylor, 10
You can tell if someone is a friend if they like you for who you are. As a boy, a girl can be your friend if you don't have a crush on her.

Melinda, 12
Real friends stay with you through thick and thin. You can trust people who like you for who you really are. I keep my old friends by talking to them nicely. You can tell if someone's a true friend because they'll like you for who you are and not what you have.

Ashlyn, 10

I've always been pretty good at picking good friends. This year I've had some faulty friendships.

Lizzie and Kate are not big fans of each other, but in the long run I think they'll come through for one another.

Heather, 10

Sometimes friends can be more than friends. Friends that I have known almost all my life I can trust. You can keep your old friends by saying sorry and making up with them. You can tell someone is a good friend if they are always there for you.

Kate used to be Lizzie's friend, and whenever Lizzie is going through something, if Kate is there Kate helps Lizzie.

I would like to have Lizzie as a really good friend.

Natalia, 11

Friends will always be there for you and help you. I can trust people who never tell or repeat gossip about me. No matter if you have other friends, you can keep your old friends by remembering how they helped you and still keep in touch.

Devin, 12

Friends are more important than anything. I stay in contact, and I can tell if someone's my friend because they invite you over and they stick up for you.

Jenny, 11

You learn that friends are what's on the inside not on the outside. You can trust your true friends and to keep them, keep your promises. As you get to know people better, you can really tell if they are good.

Your imaginary Friend

(On Friendship)

Acckk! Friends can be so flighty! But deep down, you know who your true friends are. They are the ones who kind of hunker down when you act *too* crazy—and they're still there when you come back. As Miranda says in one TV episode, "I'm happy to have the kind of friends who still care even when I'm wrong." The important thing is to make sure you don't lose your friends altogether by remembering to show them how much you really care about them. Here are some ways:

✢ Never say bad things about them to someone else, no matter how upset you are. What you say is bound to get back to them. Try writing your feelings down in a private journal instead.

✢ Remember to tell your friends what you like about them: the way they laugh, their engaging smile, or what have you. A happy friend is a good friend indeed! In one TV episode, Lizzie tells Gordo he's "smart, funny, and a little weird some- times, but I wouldn't like you any other way." Now *those* are some good pal qualities!

❀ Just because your friend isn't rich, beautiful, or
exotic doesn't mean she's not precious. True
beauty is more than skin-deep!

❀ Remember that many of your friends can, and
probably will, change. Just because someone was
your best bud in grade school doesn't mean you
will remain close to him or her in middle school
or even high school. This is natural and shouldn't
be something you need to dwell on. Look for
friends who make you feel good now, and trea-
sure each other's company and trust.

❀ If you and your closest buddies aren't speaking to
each other because of a communications break-
down or otherwise hurt feelings, try being the
first to talk. You'd be surprised how one apology
can open the floodgates to warmer feelings.

2 ✳

Embarrassing Moments

Tripping, falling, spilling . . . Lizzie does it all on her TV show and in the movie. The crème de la crème is when she trips and falls on junior high graduation day—bringing the entire stage curtain down with her in the opening scene of *The Lizzie McGuire Movie*. Thought it couldn't get worse? Never underestimate the power of a pesky little brother to put the cherry on top of that most embarrassing moment. (In the movie, Matt blackmails Lizzie by threatening to broadcast her blunder on national TV.) Other members of Lizzie's family are also experts at contributing to her humiliation. Take, for example, the time Lizzie set off on her first school field trip campout, only to find out that the last-minute chaperone was none other than her own well-meaning mother! To make matters worse, her mom showed up holding a mesh bag brimming full of toilet paper—just in case Lizzie or her friends needed it for calls of nature. Like, SO not cool!

While it seems possible that such a horribly embarrassing scene could only happen to Lizzie McGuire, many a tween can vouch for equally humiliating experiences.

KiDS' COMMENTS:

Ashlyn, 10

On one TV show, Lizzie fell headfirst into a garbage can because she wasn't paying attention. It was hilarious!

I can relate to Lizzie's embarrassing moments: Once I went to scare my friend Alexis, and it turned out it wasn't her!

What might Lizzie learn from such a situation? Don't hide from the whole world. If people tease you, act like you meant to ruin your graduation.

Elise, 12

One of my favorite embarrassing scenes from a Lizzie TV show was when Lizzie walked up to Miranda and then Miranda opened her locker and hit Lizzie in the face.

I like the show because it deals with things that happen in real life and are funny because Lizzie is so clumsy. I'm very clumsy, too! Once I was walking down the street to go see a movie, and I tripped and almost fell on my face. That was embarrassing because it was in public. I wasn't really hurt though—I just kind of stubbed my toe.

Courtney, 12

I think that all of Lizzie's trips and falls are funny—I don't have a favorite one.

I have plenty of embarrassing experiences myself, like the time I fell out of my desk in the middle of class. Like Lizzie, I am a klutz.

If you are caught in an embarrassing situation, act like nothing happened. It always works for me!

Cody, 12

My favorite embarrassing scene in the movie is when Lizzie falls in the bathtub.

Once I was at school and I knew my mother was there. I went to go hug her and—oops!—I hugged the wrong mommy.

If something embarrassing happens, just say, "Oops," and move on with your life.

❀   ❀   ❀

In an opening scene of The Lizzie McGuire Movie, *Lizzie is so busy singing to herself in the bathroom that she accidentally trips and falls (with her clothes on) into the bathtub. The scene is typical of Lizzie and her frequent bouts with clumsiness—and it's what endears her to fellow klutz fans worldwide!*

Taylor, 10

I always like when Lizzie does things like falling down. Once I had a starring role in a play, and I forgot my lines—that was embarrassing! It helps to laugh at them. You can also forget about it.

❈ ❈ ❈

No matter how many times Lizzie trips and falls, she always manages to pick herself back up again and usually with a half-silly smile. How's that for inspiration?

Morgan, 11

I tripped on the soccer field once. That was embarrassing!

Laura, 10

Once in the lunchroom someone said, "You have Pooh on your shirt," and I freaked out, but she just meant Pooh *Bear*. Embarrassing things happen when you least expect it!

Paulina, 11

Lizzie's funniest embarrassing scene to me was one time when she fell over while trying on clothes.

❈ ❈ ❈

Do clothes make the person? See what other kids think in the "Fashion Smarts" chapter.

Jenny, 11

The funniest embarrassing scene to me is when Lizzie was at school and she got hit by her locker door and fell down.

Once I was standing up raising my hand to tell the

teacher the answer. She called on me, and I told her the answer. After I told the class the answer, she told me my belt was unbuckled in front of the whole class!

What I've learned from Lizzie? When you get embarrassed, don't make everyone know it. You can feel it inside, but on the outside just smile and laugh. Then no one will make fun of you.

Merissa, 10

I went out for ice cream once and got chocolate ice cream on my face, and a guy waved to me and I waved back with chocolate on my face!

✿ ✿ ✿

Isn't this just the kind of thing that would happen to Lizzie?

Morgen, 11

I thought it was funniest when Lizzie fell in the garbage can. My own most embarrassing experience was when I farted in class.

✿ ✿ ✿

Talk about embarrassing! Morgen's experience is understandably so humiliating they'd hardly dare to show such an episode on TV. Though surely it's happened . . .

Katilyn, 13

To me Lizzie's most embarrassing scene is from the movie when she's famous and gets out of the limo to go to the concert and she starts walking and falls in front of everyone.

Once I was on a field trip and we were eating lunch, and I went to stand up and my foot got caught in the chair and I fell in front of everyone. I was so embarrassed!

If you do something embarrassing, just say, "I am OK, and you don't need to get on my case about what just happened."

❖ ❖ ❖

Embarrassing things don't just happen to the rich and famous!

Maddie, 11

I liked when, in the movie, Lizzie is walking down a carpet in the stadium and she trips. It was funny. Sometimes I trip, too.

Once I fell off a horse. My friends who ride with me saw it, so I was embarrassed. (I wasn't really hurt though.)

Nicole P., 10

I thought it was so funny on the TV show when Lizzie wore some new, favorite pants to school, and then she bumped into the janitor. When she slipped, a frozen drink got spilled all over her pants. I've had embarrassing moments, too, like the time I had to read my report in front of my class, and I was shaking.

Kameron, 11

I like the scene in the movie when Lizzie is walking down the red carpet to perform in a concert and trips in front of everyone. Once I was walking around with my friend at the mall and all of a sudden I couldn't see her. I yelled her name, and it turns out she was right behind me.

If you get into an embarrassing situation, it helps to just act like it was a joke (like Lizzie might do).

Sarah, 11

I think the funniest episode is when Lizzie gets caught in a trash can. She seems to fall into trash cans a lot—she's really a klutz!

One thing that was embarrassing to me was when I wore unmatching socks to school.

You can make a joke over what you've done to recover from an embarrassing situation.

Kaley, 11

The best way for me to avoid or recover from embarrassing situations is to laugh it off, like Lizzie does sometimes. Usually, for me, my friends are all watching me when I am embarrassed; and if I get mad at them for laughing at me, they will get mad at me, so just laugh with them, even if you don't think it is funny. If you are hurt though, you should tell them.

Sy, 12

One of my most embarrassing times was when I asked a girl out. She isn't allowed to date, but instead of saying that, she yelled, "No!" and all the kids around started to laugh.

I learned that it's best to keep your mouth shut. It's better to stand there and be called a freak instead of opening your mouth and removing all doubt.

❖   ❖   ❖

Having a crush on someone can make you especially susceptible to embarrassment in front of him or her. Just watch how frazzled Lizzie and some of her other girlfriends get on the TV show when they're around junior high school hunk Ethan Craft. As "Toon Lizzie" might advise, "Maintain face, Lizzie: deep breaths!"

Brigid, 12

One funny thing Lizzie did once on the TV show that was really embarrassing was when she ran into a book stand and then fell onto the floor because she was so busy talking about Ethan Craft. And another time she wasn't paying attention and fell into a trash can.

One embarrassing thing for me was when I was at a dance competition and was really nervous! I was on a raised stage and got so nervous I fell off the stage!

The best thing to do in that kind of situation is to just laugh and say something like, "That was graceful, wasn't it?" Or, "I had to practice for weeks. Don't try that at home!"

Mary, 10

I think it's funny when Lizzie falls in the bathtub in the movie.

Once I didn't pay attention to what was going on at our softball game. Then when everyone walked off the field, I was the only one left. That was embarrassing!

It helps to ignore what everyone else says and ask them, "Have *you* had an embarrassing moment?"

Karyssa, 12

Lizzie's scene that was embarrassing to me was at graduation when she pulls the curtain down. I thought it was funny, but I also felt really bad for Lizzie. I can relate to her embarrassment: Once I went down an alpine slide and my sandals flew off. By the time I got to the bottom I had started crying, and I had to walk around without shoes for a while. It was *sooo* embarrassing! A way to recover from embarrassing situations is to either laugh with everyone else or ignore it, like Lizzie did in the movie when she was walking into the concert and tripped.

Devin, 7

I fell off a swing once. That was really embarrassing. I wanted to leave or go hide.

✿　✿　✿

As Lizzie's cartoon alter ego says in one TV episode, "Go back, do over, rewind!" Don't we all wish we had a rewind button!

Heather, 10

I thought it was funny in the movie when Lizzie was walking down the aisle to the concert with Paolo, and she tripped. My own embarrassing experience is when I tripped in front of a boy that I like . . . but I don't like him now.

You should just leave embarrassing things in the past and go on with your life.

Ashley, 11

The embarrassing moment of Lizzie's that I like best is the time in her movie when she trips and knocks over the curtain at graduation.

My tip: Always act as if it wasn't a big deal. If you make a big deal of it, then other people will.

Emilie, 9

I like the scene when Lizzie accidentally pulls down the curtain during her graduation! When everyone watches you, it can be embarrassing—like the time I was playing tag, and I ran into one of the tetherball poles and the boy I liked was watching me when I fell.

Your imaginary Friend
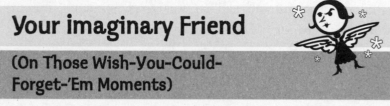

(On Those Wish-You-Could-Forget-'Em Moments)

You break out into hives just thinking about it; you wish you could dive into a hole and never come out. Erase your past; start anew. Oh, if only life were like a big blackboard!

The fact is, embarrassing stuff happens. Just like in life. So since you must live with it, we offer some tips on getting by—in spite of yourself—here:

❋ Laugh at yourself. Your friends and classmates will undoubtedly admire you for your ability to rise above embarrassment with a keen sense of humor. In the *Lizzie McGuire* TV show, even the actors laugh at themselves when the show is done, as seen in their acting "bloopers" shared with viewers in the last minutes of the show.

❋ Remember that *everyone* does embarrassing things from time to time.

❋ If you still flush just thinking about something you did or said, try to focus instead on what you *learned* from it.

❋ Put the embarrassment behind you. Use what you learned in anticipating a more confident, successful, *fab* you.

3 ✳

My Parents Drive Me Crazy!

Lizzie's dad quotes Shakespeare at critical moments . . . such as when her best buds are hanging around in clear earshot. At home, he paints garden elf sculptures and has been known to sport a flowered apron while grilling (or, to be more accurate, *burning*) steaks on the home barbecue. *Not cool.* Lizzie McGuire's mom, meanwhile, insists her junior high schooler wear a unicorn sweater on school picture day rather than something with, say, sparkles and baby blue ruffles. *Way not cool.* Who wouldn't be worried she's going to win the *dorkerella* award of the year for having the nerdiest parents on the face of the earth?

Perhaps your own parents do something as ridiculously simple as wearing Birkenstock sandals to the movies with you—which only serve to reveal their big old unmanicured toes as they rest them up on the seat in front of you. Or they insist on treating you like a baby when it's been *years* since kindergarten, let alone the days when you wore diapers. Come *on!*

They seem so clueless sometimes: They see all too clearly your clothes, nail polish, and hair spray bottles strewn across your room as if a random "tornado" hit it, but they *don't* seem to see beyond their crazy rectangular glasses—to how you're feeling—that is, pestered, ignored, or just generally *freaked out.* What to do?

One thing to remember, however, is that your parents aren't just dreary old folks. Cut them some slack, and they can be fun and silly, too. It's heartwarming, for example, to see in one Lizzie TV episode that her parents challenge each other to a pillow fight, raid the fridge, and build forts for fun together one day when both their kids are out. "I'm so glad I married you," says Lizzie's mom to her dad. *Cute!*

KiDS' COMMENTS:

Taylor, 10

When my parents say, "Clean up your room," or, "Don't pick on your brother," it drives me crazy.

To make things better, it helps to just improve in the areas they bother you about, so they'll leave you alone.

✷　✷　✷

Messy rooms and brothers who bug you to the point of frustration are a normal part of any preteen's life—as are the parents who get on your case about these kinds of things. Every now and then, however, even Lizzie's alter-ego cartoon character manages to rise above it all, saying things like, "Now this is why I love my parents" (at times when they bail you out of a scary predicament or other sticky situation, for example). Remembering these moments of appreciation can help you get through all those other drive-you-crazy times.

Karyssa, 12

Sometimes when I want to do something and my parents won't let me, it really annoys me.

I think just talking to your parents and explaining why you want to do something will usually help. If they won't let you do something, explain to them that you're mature enough to handle it.

Ashlyn, 10

Mostly my parents embarrass me in front of my friends.

When they drive you crazy, it helps to just tell your parents you need to be alone for a while.

Devin, 12

My parents say, "Clean this," and, "Clean that."

Maybe it would help to sit down and talk to your parents and ask your mom to take you out to lunch and just talk it over.

✤　✤　✤

In one TV episode, Lizzie even invites her mom with her to have a drink at the Sugar Bean café. While her friends think she's crazy, Lizzie ends up having a conversation with her mom unlike any other she's had before.

Laura, 10

Oh yeah, my parents drive me crazy sometimes . . . like when they tell me I can't wear something or see certain movies or listen to a song. . . .

My way to work it out: Push, push until they finally give in!

❋ ❋ ❋

Like most parents, Lizzie's mom and dad usually stand by their decisions no matter how much you push them. And usually, you'll find there's a good reason behind their decision. Take, for instance, the time Lizzie lied to her parents, telling them she was going to the mall when she really went to an unchaperoned party that her parents didn't want her going to. Without a chaperone, the party turned into a disaster. Luckily, in this case, Lizzie fessed up to her mom by calling her before things got too out of control.

Sy, 12

Sometimes my parents act like babies. One way to make things work with them is to agree with everything they say.

Cody, 12

My parents drive me crazy sometimes. The thing that drives me crazy the most is when my parents tell me to clean my room. To work things out with your parents, just tell them the truth. If you are angry, upset, or worried about something, just come clean.

❊   ❊   ❊

Lizzie's room is anything but clean. Hair spray bottles, nail polish, clothes strewn across every piece of furniture . . . It's nice to see a room like that on a TV set because it's realistic and shows kids something they can relate to.

Natalia, 11

Like Lizzie's mom and dad, my parents always tell me to do things.

My advice: Don't hide things from your parents.

❊   ❊   ❊

Lizzie often learns the hard way not to hide things from her parents. In fact, by letting them in on your plans, you might discover they can be a big help. In real life, actress Hilary Duff refers to her own parents as her "greatest supporters."

Emilie, 9

My parents drive me crazy when they say weird phrases such as, "I'm such a Bat Dinger."

❊   ❊   ❊

Parents say the darndest things. Like calling you by your full name in front of your friends: "Elizabeth Brooke McGuire," rants Mrs.

Duff on the occasional TV episode. Or by trying to be cool, they say things that can only sound dorky coming from their mouths. Like, duh!

Ashley, 11

My mom always drives me crazy. When I'm in the dressing room of my dance studio she yells down there for me to hurry up. It's really annoying.

Melinda, 12

My parents won't always let me go to certain places without one of them along. I've learned that you should just relax though because probably you'll do the same things one day when you're a parent yourself.

❖　❖　❖

In one TV episode, Lizzie gets a chance to play the role of a parent with her brother, Matt. That is, her mom asks her to watch Matt for the afternoon while she's out. When Matt doesn't do as she says, Lizzie learns firsthand what it feels like to be a frustrated parent: "I set the rules and he breaks them—he doesn't think of the consequences of his actions!" she vents to pal Miranda about Matt's unruliness.

Miranda's reply: "Sounding a little parental, aren't we?" Indeed!

Paulina, 11

My parents annoy me all the time 'cuz they are so freaked out about guys!

It helps to tell your parents how you feel.

Kaley, 11

My parents usually don't drive me crazy, except for the occasional, "Clean up your room!"

I don't really have to worry about not getting along with my parents, but to me, the best way to deal with this problem is to talk to your parents. Ask for a family meeting, and tell them what's on your mind. Don't be afraid to ask them to do something different.

Mary, 10

My parents drive me crazy when they tell me to pick up someone else's mess when I didn't do it.

Morgen, 11

It drives me crazy when my fourteen-year-old brother runs up the stairs singing in a high voice and my mom doesn't do anything.

❖   ❖   ❖

Perhaps even worse is when your parents actually encourage a pesky sibling to do something that bothers you. Like the way Matt's dad will sometimes try to help him in his never-ending quest to become a TV star, win a contest, or some other silly pursuit. Whatever!

Sarah, 11

My parents drive me crazy, but it turns out they're always right.

To get along with your parents, it helps to just do what you're told. Be as good a student as you can.

Heather, 10

One thing that drives me crazy is when you ask someone to stop doing something, and they hear you but they just get louder.

Jenny, 11

What drives me crazy is when I ask for something and they say, "No!" They don't give me any freedom.

When your parents tell you, "No," when you ask for something, don't throw a fit. Just say, "OK." Then they will think you are maturing and may give you more privileges.

* * *

"They want complete and total control of my life," complains Lizzie in one TV episode, when her parents won't agree to raising her allowance. As a result, Lizzie tries getting a job. At first everything seems rosy: "I'm free—I'm independent!" she raves. But soon the job turns out to be more than she bargained for. In the end, Lizzie's dad explains things in an ever-so-sweet way: "The great thing about being a kid is that your only job is to get good grades, hang out with friends, and be a good kid—and you've got those covered."

When your own parents say, "No," to something, it might help to remember this point.

Brigid, 12

One thing that drives me crazy is when your parents get mad for no reason!

The best thing to do is to apologize or forgive and forget.

Katilyn, 13

Sometimes my parents drive me crazy. Well, like when I am asked to do something while I am trying to do something else.

One way to work things out with your parents is to go up to them and talk to them, and hope that they will understand.

Kameron, 11

Oh yeah, my parents drive me crazy sometimes: My dad is too loud, and my mom overreacts too much.

If your parents drive you crazy, just ignore them—that's what I do.

Courtney, 12

My parents are really cool. There are times when they embarrass me, but for the most part I love them.

Be honest with your parents—that's the best thing to do. Let them know their mistake, so they can make it better.

Your imaginary Friend

(On Putting Up with Parents)

"Grrrr," you grumble—angry, imaginary steam puffing from your head. "They drive me crazy!!!" Trying to remain calm when you and your parents have a disagreement is easier said than done. Sometimes their demands seem totally unreasonable and out of this world! As Lizzie says in one TV episode, when her parents tell her to do something that conflicts with her idea of a good time (like hanging with friends at the mall): "But I have plans—that's so unfair!"

The fact is, your parents—no matter how alien they sometimes seem—*are* here on earth more or less to stay. The best way to communicate with them, then:

❄ Tell it like it is. Try not to blame them for anything right off the bat; just say how their actions make *you feel*.

❄ Rather than putting them on the defensive with accusations or crying fits, try starting a conversation with your parents this way: "I love you and need you. Here's why. . . ."

❄ If they still don't seem to hear you, try writing them a note and leave it somewhere they can't miss—such as on their pillow.

❄ Can't think—let alone talk—calmly at home? Suggest the two (or three) of you spend some time alone together where you *can* talk—such as on a walk or over lunch at a restaurant. (Lizzie's been known to take her mom for a chat at the Sugar Bean café.)

❄ Prove to your parents how grown up and responsible you are by doing things like keeping up your grades, helping out around the house . . . or maybe even bringing some sense of order to that bedroom tornado.

❋ Ask your parents for the reasoning behind any decision they make that you don't understand. You will probably find they actually have your best interests in mind.

4 ✳

Copycats

imitation: the highest form of flattery? How about when your admirer takes it too far and does things like changing her hair color to match yours or spying on you? Sound familiar? If you've watched enough *Lizzie McGuire* TV episodes, you'll remember how Lizzie's cartoon alter ego goes "directly to freak out" when Lizzie is faced with just such a copycat. "I want my life back!" she laments, after a pesky "sevenny" (seventh grader) starts dressing like her, following her everywhere, and invading her personal space, including her locker and even her home.

Even scarier, perhaps, is the fact that we can probably all recall a time when we did our fair share of copying. (Hint: When you're in a fix, do you find yourself pursing and biting your lips and blinking your eyes . . . and then talking to some kind of crazy alter-ego mirror reflection?)

Actress Hilary Duff would be flattered, however: "It's cool that people might be looking up to me," she reported in a recent interview.

Even Lizzie tries to remake herself in one TV episode in order to make herself more like someone she thinks "hottie" Ethan Craft may admire. She learns, of course, that trying to be someone you're not is a sure recipe for disaster.

KiDS' COMMENTS:

Brigid, 12
Someone copied me once, and I was embarrassed and really angry!

Katilyn, 13
My sister started to copy me. At first I didn't care, but after a while you get really annoyed at them so you blow it in their face; you didn't really mean to hurt their feelings, but you did. It made me mad, but after it was over I felt really bad.

❋ ❋ ❋

Wow, I'm going to be a mentor, *thinks Lizzie at first, when an admirer starts copying her in one TV episode. She tries letting the admirer down nicely at first by saying, "You don't want to be like me—I fall down, oversleep, and trip." When the admirer doesn't take the gentle hint and keeps on copying her, however, Lizzie explodes: "Get out of my life!" she finally tells the girl.*

As Lizzie learns how, being nice because you don't want to hurt someone's feelings doesn't always work. Tell it like it is, and your admirer may simply move on to copying someone else. (In Lizzie's case, her admirer moved on to copying Kate—Ha!)

Sy, 12

Copycats are OK at first, but really annoying after that.

I've never copied someone else. I'm an individual.

Laura, 10

My little sister copies me all the time, and it drives me nuts! I've never copied anyone because I've always thought I was good as myself.

Heather, 10

Copycats bother me so much. Once I did copy someone else for "Twin Day" at school when you pick a friend you want to match. And it just made me feel that you were matching your best friend.

Kaley, 11

From what I remember, no one has ever copied me. I've never copied anyone either, and if I did, I would feel like a copycat.

Melinda, 12

Copycats make me feel annoyed because I feel like I do everyone's schoolwork.

✻ ✻ ✻

Copying someone's schoolwork—or letting someone copy your work—
can both be dangerous to your school career. Take, for example, the
TV episode when Angel copies Lizzie's schoolwork in class. Both girls
end up getting detention. Yikes!

Sarah, 11

I've had someone copy me. I didn't like it until I noticed
they're just doing it because they like you or your ideas.

I've never copied anyone in the way they dress because
I like my way.

Taylor, 10

Copycats drive me nuts!

Kameron, 11

When someone copies you, it makes you feel too close to
whoever's copying you.

I've never copied someone else because I know how annoying it is.

❀ ❀ ❀

Gordo puts it well on the TV episode about a "sevenny" copying
Lizzie: "She wears you well," he observes. The idea drives Lizzie
crazy, to the point where she has an equally crazy nightmare that
brings Gordo's observation to "life." Way freaky!

Courtney, 12

If there is one thing I can't stand, it's a copycat. I think that people should be independent—I mean, I think it's great to have someone look up to you, but copycats, I think not!

Ashley, 11

I have had someone copy me. It made me feel as if my clothes and jewelry weren't really mine anymore.

Cody, 12

I felt like a great role model for people when they copied me. I have never copied anyone else.

Karyssa, 12

When people copy me, it sometimes annoys me, depending on what they are copying.

Sometimes I copy people's hairstyles or a shirt they have, but I always try not to look exactly like them because I know people don't like being copied. Also, I like to have my own style.

Natalia, 11

I've had people copy the clothes I wear. It made me feel that I was cool, but also it made me feel I'm not independent.

I don't want to copy other people, so I change it so it's like my own creation.

Your imaginary Friend

(On Copycats)

Meow! Who said copycats aren't cute . . . for a while? When they go beyond admiring to obsessing, however, you know it's time to do something.

❅ Speak up. That doesn't mean purr gently. It means tell your admirer outright that you don't feel comfortable being in such a spotlight.

❅ Mirror their actions. Flattering your admirer with compliments on unique traits of *theirs* just might help them stop obsessing about *you*.

❅ If they go so far as to copy something like your *homework,* suggest you study together (if you can stand encouraging that much "together" time), and explain that you don't think it's fair for only one person to do all the work.

5 ✳

The Popularity Contest

opularity, schmopularity. Have you ever wondered what's the big deal about being popular? Take a peek at your dictionary, and you'll find it comes from the Latin word *popularis,* meaning "of the people." When applied to Lizzie's former grade-school-pal-turned-snobby-cheerleader Kate, the word takes on new meaning—that is, "*above* the people." Kate's superiority complex does little more than make Lizzie's existence at Hillridge Junior High miserable. It's not until she gets her own movie that Lizzie seems to finally live her dreams—that is, when she takes the stage at the Roman Colosseum and croons un-abashedly to the crowd. (We're talking *thousands* of scream-ing fans. *Way* popular!)

To most junior high schoolers and tweens, being pop-ular isn't quite so glamorous—it simply means fitting in *somehow, somewhere*—whether that means the cheerleaders' lunch table or hangin' with the chess club.

And then there are those devastating, not-so-popular stereotypes. Take nerdy Larry on the Lizzie TV show: His nose-picking, Klingon-speaking habits lead to his exclusion from many a crowd at school, to the point that even Miranda decides not to invite him to her party. Here's where Lizzie's "inner voice" kicks in, resulting in her feeling sensitive to Larry's left-out feelings. Oddness aside, she realizes, he can be a pretty cool guy.

If you saw the episode, you'll recall how Lizzie gives Larry a makeover, complete with new clothes, cool shades, and a slick hairdo to help him fit in. When he shows up at Miranda's party, Miranda doesn't recognize him and begins to flirt with the mysterious cutie.

Soon Lizzie's not the only one whose conscience kicks in: Even Miranda comes around and realizes her mistake. "Larry shouldn't have to disguise himself," she admits. "I was so caught up in having the perfect party that I forgot to act like a human being."

That's what we all are, after all: human beings, characterized by strengths and weaknesses that make each one of us unique. It's something to remember in the quest for popularity.

KiDS' COMMENTS:

Karyssa, 12

I don't think I'm popular like Kate is on the show, but I think a lot of people like me because I try to be nice to everyone. It matters to me to be liked by everyone and to look cool, but I don't feel I have to be the coolest kid in school.

People fit in by being nice and funny and by dressing cool!

Heather, 10

Am I popular? No, I sort of feel like I'm in the middle, like Lizzie.

Jenny, 11

It doesn't really matter to me to be popular, but I do want everyone to like me.

At my school kids are popular when they wear cool clothes, shoes, etc.

Paulina, 11

A person is popular at my school by trying not to act weird.

Laura, 10

Yes, I'm very popular. Sometimes it's good to be popular but not always! The way you become popular is by having friends and having people respect you.

Devin, 12

It's not important to me to be popular because some people won't like you just because you're popular.

At my school kids are popular if they dress good or have a good personality or they're nice.

Ashley, 11

I don't feel like I am popular, but I don't care. I already have plenty of friends.

Emilie, 9

Yes, I feel like I am popular. Almost whatever I do or say, my friends do it also. Someone becomes popular if everyone starts to copy them or have ten or more friends who play with them every day.

Courtney, 12

It doesn't matter to me about being popular. I think that people should overlook the way you dress or the way you do your hair. People should like you for who you are.

At my school kids fit in by being themselves. At my school most people like you for who you are.

Dylan, 8

If you're really cool and everyone wants to be your friend, you're popular. I think the way you dress is one reason.

Nicole P., 10

People normally become popular when they are good-looking.

Katilyn, 13

I don't really feel like I am popular, but I don't mind it. If you have friends, then that is good enough for me.

Or you would have to wear Limited Too brand clothes.

Morgen, 11

Someone is popular when they hang out with the popular people.

Cody, 12

I feel like I am popular, but it does not matter to me if I am popular.

A kid fits in by being nice or by what they wear. Also, they fit in by smelling good.

Merissa, 10

Being popular does not matter to me at all. I hate some people who are popular!

❀   ❀   ❀

While Lizzie's cartoon alter ego isn't shy about expressing frustration or anger toward rivals like Kate, in reality she rarely voices such strong opinions. Talking to a friend, parent, or teacher about your feelings can usually help you to express your feelings. (Lizzie does this a lot!) Or it can help to try focusing on other, more productive activities, like taking a nice long bike ride, drawing a picture, or singing along to a favorite song on the radio (but don't get so carried away that you fall into a bathtub like Lizzie!).

Sarah, 11

I don't feel popular, but I don't care. I'm a good student who tries to be as best and nice as I can to other people, so I shouldn't care.

To be popular some kids act silly and are friends with the most popular one.

Taylor, 10

At my school a kid who is popular gets a lot of rewards.

Ashlyn, 10

At my school kids are popular if they weigh less than eighty pounds and/or are good at sports.

❈   ❈   ❈

While the actress Hilary Duff is a beautiful girl, fans may note that she definitely weighs more than eighty pounds!

Kameron, 11

I don't feel like I'm popular, but I have a lot of friends. It doesn't matter to me to be popular. Why should it?

A kid fits in or is popular at my school by what they wear.

Brigid, 12

I'm sort of popular in my inner circle but not in the outer! To be popular at school in general you have to be the cheerleader type.

✿ ✿ ✿

Though there's nothing wrong with cheerleaders, per se, they do get a bad rap thanks to snobby Kate's supportive squadron of cheerleader pals. Uh-huh!

Kaley, 11

I don't feel like I am popular because everyone else just refers to me as "the girl who reads too much." A kid is popular at my school by how they dress, how they act, and who they hang out with.

✳ ✳ ✳

Lizzie likes to read a lot, too. In one TV episode, Lizzie has a school reading project where she's inspired by the story of a close relationship between a mother and daughter. As a result, Lizzie decides she wants to be closer to her own mother, too. What she ends up learning, however, is that the imaginary world of reading isn't always so ideal: Being close to her mom is one thing—but being too close and learning too much can often be totally annoying.

Your imaginary Friend

(She's So Popular . . . Or *Not?*)

Popular: There's that word again—eek! If only we didn't have to worry about what anyone else thinks.

Here's some good news: You don't have to. The first step

to being popular is being popular with *yourself.* Lizzie's
teacher, Mr. Dig, puts it well in one episode where he's trying to reassure Gordo that he's OK no matter how tall (or
short) he is: "When I decided that being short didn't matter
to me, it didn't matter to anyone else either."

No matter what you feel your flaw is (short legs, big nose,
wide hips, knobby elbows, pimples, kinky hair, freckles . . .
you name it!), just remember Mr. Dig's advice: When you
get over it, everyone else will, too.

So once you're over it, then what? You can start winning
friends who like you for your best, shining qualities (and
they will shine once you've stopped smudging them with
your other hang-ups). Just imagine: You'll be the most popular kid around! (In your circle anyway because who cares
about anybody else's?)

6 ✳

Fashion Smarts

in one magazine interview, actress Hilary Duff claims she's at liberty to choose most of the outfits she wears on her TV show. No doubt about it, the "tween queen" is a trendsetter, but not in a cookie-cutter way. Her style is so whimsical that one day you may see her in baby blue ruffles, hip huggers, and ringlet locks tucked under a red cowboy scarf; or the next day you might see her in a tailored, cuffed jacket with chunky shoes, a rhinestone belt, sparkly eye shadow, and hair teased up in a *I Dream of Jeannie* look. And almost every time you see Lizzie, she's wearing a heart-shaped charm dangling from her neck, lending an innocent, sweet quality to her otherwise quirky wardrobe. *Way cute!*

Overall, Lizzie seems to have fun with fashion rather than be a slave to it. Just as a young girl might have fun dressing a doll in different outfits (and don't forget there is actually a Lizzie fashion doll on the market!), Lizzie the TV and movie star isn't afraid to try new combinations. Lizzie's outfits have even inspired several lines of clothing in the stores, as well as Lizzie-themed accessories like pink-feather-covered school binders (as seen in one TV episode) and cartoon-Lizzie diaries.

What's more, according to one report, Hilary Duff's passion for fashion extends to her pets: Her fox terrier–Chihuahua mix Little Dog sports a rhinestone collar!

KiDS' COMMENTS:

Bailey, 11
I like Lizzie's clothes and her personality. She's spunky and her clothes stand out—they're different than what you usually see. I do know people who try to dress like her.

Emilie, 9
I like the outfit Lizzie's wearing when she is singing on stage in a concert with Isabella.

❋ ❋ ❋

After first trying on numerous gaudy outfits in preparation for her Roman Colosseum debut in The Lizzie McGuire Movie, *Lizzie finally appears in front of the crowd in an eye-popping outfit featuring a finely tailored, cuffed jacket, navel-baring, fabulous bell-bottoms (under a removable, magnificent skirt), and scintillating sparkly eye shadow. In this case, Lizzie is definitely not an "outfit repeater"! It's the stuff dreams are made of!*

Laura, 10

My favorite outfit is actually not Lizzie's but Isabella's in *The Lizzie McGuire Movie.*

❋ ❋ ❋

Did you know the character of Isabella in the movie is played by none other than Hilary Duff herself? How's that for an alter ego? Though more exotic, what with her experienced stardom and foreign accent, Isabella turns out to be just as nice, deep down, as Lizzie. Her style is like Lizzie's, too, only more sophisticated. Thanks to camera tricks, the "pair" make a dynamic, dazzling duo.

Katilyn, 13

I love all of Lizzie's outfits, but I couldn't pick one that's my favorite. I have been inspired by her in that I now realize you don't have to be perfect to be a good friend.

❋ ❋ ❋

None of Lizzie's outfits is perfect, in the sense that it matches perfectly. While rival Kate is known for wearing all-too-perfect cashmere sweater sets, Lizzie's mix-and-match style makes her more realistic and endearing to fans.

Courtney, 12

A favorite Lizzie outfit? I do not have just one Lizzie outfit. I think all of her clothes are fab!

Ashlyn, 10

I really like the outfit Lizzie wore the first day of eighth grade, in the TV episode when the "sevenny" tried to copy her. She wore a peach-colored, ruffled blouse and a denim short skirt. It looked really pretty on Lizzie. She also had her hair in funky braids all tied up in a bun with a flower and a headband and clips. When I'm older I might wear an outfit like that. In the meantime, I wear different stuff— Lizzie has taught me to be me.

Amanda, 10

I really like Lizzie because she's pretty—but also because she's very pretty, smart, and intelligent. I wish I could be like her sometimes!

✽ ✽ ✽

Amanda makes a good observation: Winning fashion and beauty aren't all in the looks; sometimes they're in the smarts of a person!

Nicole P., 10

When she wore her new pants, they really looked good on her.

✽ ✽ ✽

Lizzie's goal in one TV episode is to win the "Best Dressed" prize in a contest at school. "All you have to do is be better dressed than Kate or Claire for one day—and you'll be best dressed in the yearbook forever!" says Gordo. In search of the most "outrageously hip outfit," Lizzie ends up pooling money with her friends and spending top dollar for a pair of hip huggers. The pants are, indeed, outrageously fab, but not so much after Lizzie trips on the janitor's broom at school and spills an iced drink all over them . . . and to top it off, someone takes a picture of it. Claire ends up winning the contest after all, but the lesson Lizzie learns is invaluable. As the TV theme song goes, ". . . we figure it out our own way."

Maddie, 11

I'm not really into fashion, but I like when she just wears jeans and a shirt. I like sportswear like that.

Melinda, 12

I like Lizzie's outfit on the "best-dressed day" with her bargain pants. You don't always have to have the most expensive clothes to look good; just be yourself and have your own trends.

Sarah, 11

I don't like Lizzie's clothes. I like plain clothes: tennis shoes, jeans, shirt, and sweater.

Brigid, 12

My favorite outfit of Lizzie's? ALL OF THEM!!! She has a great wardrobe. She inspired me to be me.

Kameron, 11

I haven't been inspired by Lizzie's clothes because I'm a boy, and I wear boys' clothes . . . duh!

Cody, 12

I don't have a favorite outfit of Lizzie's; I love them all.

Karyssa, 12

I like some of the outfits she wore in the movie. I have been inspired by them because she has her own cool style. I have been inspired by her in the movie because she went out and did something and became someone.

Jenny, 11

What inspires me is that Lizzie just wears what she wants and has fun with it. I don't have a favorite outfit of hers.

Annabel, 8

I think it's really cool the way Miranda puts her hair up in all sorts of braids, buns, and pigtails. I don't wear my hair that way myself, but I like the way it looks on her.

Dylan, 8

Fashion is what I like most about Lizzie. I think it's really cool. The outfit she wore to the concert in the movie was one of my favorites—she was wearing a big fluffy skirt with pants under it and a little purple shirt under a coat. Her hair was hanging down and curly. She had a charm necklace

I think, and she put sparkly eye shadow on. I put some on like that for Halloween when I was dressed up like an angel. Lizzie's always wearing different things. I like to dress like her. She makes me want to go to the mall and get her clothes.

Your imaginary Friend

(On Style Matters)

"Born to shop!" Do you sometimes wish you had a sticker on your backpack with that motto? Or would you just as soon get by with the bare essentials?

As Lizzie learns in one TV episode, you don't need to shop at the hippest (and priciest) shop in town to win the best-dressed award at school. Taking your time to hit the "bargain basement" could yield many more mix-and-match hip outfits than one pair of hip huggers at Chez Chic. And you will probably have more fun while you're at it. After Lizzie had to change out of her expensive, soiled hip huggers into the bargain pair her mom had bought for her at half the cost, Lizzie realized, "By the end of the day everyone wanted to know where I got them. I wish I could go shopping with you next time!"

The key to good fashion sense is, indeed, to *have fun with it.* You could even swap with friends and try using your accessories in different ways to extend the life of them. As Lizzie puts it in *The Lizzie McGuire Movie,* "Jewelry: Now that's a language every girl understands!" But it doesn't have to be the real stuff. Sparkly faux gems and glittery plastic beads (nothing tacky, of course) can be a lot more fun—and cheap—to mix and match. And don't forget to check the stores for some of Hilary's own accessory lines! Hello, fabulous!

7 ✳

On Bullies and Bravery

How to define a bully? For her relentlessly flippant mocking of Lizzie, the shiny-peach-lip-gloss-wearing, matching-sweater-set type, Kate, frequently falls into that category. Often Lizzie doesn't have the courage to stand up to the snobby cheerleader. Fortunately, she has pals Miranda and Gordo to stick up for her when she's feeling not-so-confident.

The funny thing is, the reason most bullies act so mean or tease others is because they are feeling not so good about *themselves.* Picking on someone is a way they've found to make themselves feel more important. They might grab your stuff, make fun of you, or purposefully leave you out. Or they might force you to do something you don't want to do. Often, as a victim, you might feel embarrassed or scared.

KiDS' COMMENTS:

Cody, 12

Kate is just really rude and likes herself too much.

If someone is being bullied, tell that person to say, "Thanks for thinking of me," and walk away.

✾ ✾ ✾

Walking away with an arrogant flip of your hair is something we can all learn from one bully herself: Kate. Leaving out the arrogant part, however, might be advisable!

Bailey, 11

I think Ms. Ungermeyer in the Lizzie movie is kind of a bully. She doesn't have faith in people.

Ashlyn, 10

Kate is mean to Lizzie all the time. So is Angel. I think they are jealous of Lizzie and are under a lot of peer pressure.

To deal with bullies, I have learned a method in a bully-proofing class at my school: "*H*elp *A*ssert *H*umor *A*void *S*elf-talk *O*wn it" (also known as "Ha-Ha, So!"). That is, ask for *H*elp if you're being bullied. *A*ssert yourself if you're being bullied by standing up for yourself or other people you see being bullied. If someone makes fun of you, use *H*umor by laughing at yourself too to distract the bully and make them stop. *A*void bullies. And use *S*elf-talk to boost yourself up—

like if someone calls you something mean, tell yourself not to listen to them. And *O*wn it, by saying to yourself, "OK, so what if they call me 'four eyes'; they're not perfect either and have no right to make fun of me."

✻   ✻   ✻

Out of all of the tips we learn from Ashlyn, the one that we've seen work best for Lizzie is "Humor." Laughing at yourself and the situation can do totally awesome wonders for your self-esteem!

Taylor, 10
Don't listen to bullies. If they say, "That dress is ugly," pretend to agree with them.

Paulina, 11
Kate is a bully, but she only bullies by words.

Morgen, 11
If someone bullies you, just walk away.

Emilie, 9
Lizzie was bullied in the TV episode when Kate was in charge of Halloween and told her to do almost everything that's gross. Kate bosses her around all the time.

Jenny, 11
Just don't take what bullies say seriously because they are just jealous of you.

Katilyn, 13

Kate is always mean to Lizzie when she sees her in school. But she's not a bully when they aren't at school.

If someone is a bully, you should just go up to a teacher or a parent and tell them that so-and-so is bothering you and ask them if they can watch the bully for you or check up on you.

Melinda, 12

Kate really is a good person but just wants to stay popular, and for some reason everyone likes her stupid attitude.

Whatever you do with a bully, don't fight back. Walk away and the person won't feel as tough.

Kameron, 11

Everybody's nice to me—I've never been bullied. I don't think Lizzie is bullied by Kate, but she is made fun of by her. Kate is just rude and into herself.

Brigid, 12

Almost all the boys at my school are bullies. A bully is someone who takes their problems out on someone else. If you just ignore a bully, they will leave.

✿ ✿ ✿

Sometimes boys will tease girls because they're just as nervous about making friends with them as girls are the other way around. Though it doesn't necessarily mean they are bullies, it can be troublesome or even hurtful. After her ex-boyfriend Ronny says something hurtful

*to her in one TV episode, long-time good pal Gordo offers Lizzie
some sweet advice: "Forget about Ronny—he doesn't deserve you."
True friends who care about each other—no matter whether they're
girls or boys—can say the nicest things!*

Kaley, 11

I've met a bully, and I didn't like it very much. A bully ac-
cuses you of doing and saying things you didn't do or say.

I don't think Kate is a bully; I just think she has a very
rude way of expressing her feelings to Lizzie.

The only advice I can offer to kids who are being bullied
is to ask the bully in a nice way to stop.

Karyssa, 12

Lizzie was bullied in almost every episode with Kate in it. I
think Kate is a bully because she is always putting people
down.

To deal with a bully, you can either ignore them or try
to be nice to them and become their friend.

❊　❊　❊

*Be careful whom you befriend, however. As Lizzie learns in one
episode, being friends with bully-ish Angel isn't the best choice.*

Sy, 12

Stay away from bullies. If you can't, tell a teacher or parent.

Courtney, 12

In a lot of the episodes where Lizzie has encounters with Kate, Lizzie has been bullied. I have met bullies before, but I have never had a bad experience with one.

Kate is definitely a bully. I think that anyone who is bossy, mean, and goes out of their way to make someone's life miserable is a bully. Kate is always mean and bossy.

If you are being bullied, try to be a good example. Don't start talking back or they will continue to bully you.

Heather, 10

Lizzie was bullied by Kate when she was having picture day, and Kate made fun of her. Kate picks on everyone she hates. I have met bullies, but luckily I have never had to really deal with them.

❊   ❊   ❊

In one TV episode, Lizzie faces a "clothing emergency" when her parents pressure her into wearing a dorky unicorn sweater on school picture day. Even worse is when snobby ex-friend Kate teases Lizzie for wearing the same thing twice. The show explores Lizzie's comical attempt to come up with a new outfit. Oh, if only we all had a spare, totally fabulous and unrepeated outfit in our backpack for emergencies like this one!

Sarah, 11

When Lizzie got teased by Kate about her clothes, I think Lizzie was being bullied. Kate shouldn't pick on people like that.

If someone bullies you, ignore them, and if someone else is being bullied, tell someone.

Your imaginary Friend

(On Big Bad Bullies)

"Why's everybody always picking on me?" goes an old song. It's how many of us feel from time to time, especially when we're not sure who the bully *is*.

As eleven-year-old contributor Bailey points out, sometimes even a teacher can be a bully. (Recall the "scary headset woman," Ms. Ungermeyer, in the Lizzie movie, who orders all the kids around like a drill sergeant? She's so intent on yelling into her amplifier headset as the kids tour around Rome that she fails to hear what's really going on with the kids.) If someone is bullying you like that, be sure to talk to your friends, another adult, or your parents about it. (You may even have to speak up quite loudly to be heard!)

Sometimes bullies are the very people you try, for some odd reason, to be friends with. If a group of kids act stuck up toward you, or are otherwise unkind to you, why not focus your attention on making some newer, nicer friends elsewhere? Try joining a club (dance, music, yearbook, sports, or whatever!) to meet some new pals who make you feel good rather than bad.

Tell bullies outright that you don't appreciate being called names or being treated a certain way. The longer you let them treat you badly, the more readily they'll see you as an easy scapegoat.

One way to build up your courage to stand up to a bully is to practice role playing in front of a mirror or even with your parents at home. Have them pretend to be a bully in a similar situation, and you tell them how you feel about it.

Another way to avoid being bullied is to do like Lizzie: Buddy up with some good pals. A bully is less likely to pick on you if friends surround you.

By standing up for yourself, or telling an adult if that doesn't work, you'll not only help yourself but help a bully learn they need to change their behavior if *they* want to have more friends.

8 ✱

The Real Hilary Duff

She's quirky; she's cute; she's adorable. The best part about Lizzie, as her thousands of fans will attest, is that she's far from perfect: She slips on spilt Slurpees and finds herself in all kinds of embarrassing predicaments.

As a fictional character, fans obviously find Lizzie's blend of earnest silliness irresistible. But what about the actress behind the character? With her public image so tied to the character of "Lizzie," one wonders just who Hilary really is.

We do know that "Hil" (as her pals call her) enjoys doing many of the same things as her character: "Just hangin' with friends" is her favorite hobby listed on the official Hilary Duff fan site: www.hilaryduff.com. She also reportedly treasures spending time with her family (which, by the way, is a bit different from her TV characters), including big sis, Haylie; parents, Susan and Bob Duff; and two dogs. Due to her busy schedule, the actress doesn't attend a regular school like Hillridge Junior High, but she spends hours between filmings with a homeschool tutor instead. (Her favorite subject, according to her official Web site, is world history.)

Her career as a star started out innocently enough: As a youngster growing up in Texas, she took to twirling around in a ballet tutu like many a girl her age. At age six, the ambitious dancer went professional by joining the Columbus Ballet Met touring company in a production of *The Nutcracker.* Young Hilary's endearing smile and likable style obviously caught someone's attention, and soon she was offered an opportunity to act in a TV commercial. Before long, the rising star had earned a number of TV acting credits, which eventually brought her to Hollywood along with sister, Haylie (also an actress and singer), and Mom, while Dad held down the fort in Texas.

Why Not?

Today, Hilary Duff divides her time between homes in Houston and Los Angeles, where she records TV shows, movies, and now music albums. She also jet sets around the country doing interviews for early and late shows, magazines, and newspapers. Through it all, Hilary has been fortunate to have the support of her family: "I am very supportive of my mom and dad's involvement in my career and appreciate the guidance of my management team," she quoted recently to the media.

Born September 28, 1987, Hilary is fast outgrowing her popular middle-school fictional character, yet still maintains her sense of youthful silliness—as well as Lizzie's sincerity: The singer and actress has served as an animal rights advocate as well as on various nonprofit advisory committees geared toward helping less advantaged children. In her spare time, the multitalented teen says she enjoys tumbling, swimming, practicing Tae-Bo, rollerblading, and doing yo-yo tricks. Hilary's popular single from *The Lizzie McGuire Movie* sound track, "Why Not," seems to sum up this celebrity's life philosophy: Why not take a crazy chance?

The popularity of Lizzie McGuire lives on, thanks to the sixty-five episodes Hilary started filming in 2001, which continue to show regularly on the Disney Channel and its ABC-TV Network. In August 2002, Hilary added music to her repertoire, making her singing debut with her single, "I Can't Wait," on the *Lizzie McGuire* sound track, followed by a Christmas-themed album and a "Tiki Tiki Room" performance on another album by Walt Disney Records.

Hil has even tried her hand at role reversal: Playing the character called Lorraine in a movie she's filming with Steve Martin, *Cheaper by the Dozen,* the young actress gets to act the part of a, like, really *popular* girl. Way to go, Hil! In spring 2003, the actress starred in *The Lizzie McGuire Movie* from Walt Disney Pictures, and had a leading role in *Agent Cody Banks* from MGM pictures. The release of *The Lizzie McGuire Movie* sound track, including Hilary's hit singles "Why Not" and "What Dreams Are Made Of," has become *way* popular with fans. The sound track also includes a zippy song, "Girl in the Band," by Hil's big sister, Haylie.

Hilary's own album *Metamorphosis* was set to hit the racks in late summer 2003.

Even with an album in the works and impressive TV and movie credits under her belt, Hilary aspires to do something many normal kids do when they grow up: go to college. Maybe we can expect to see a TV tale about her adventures in college one day soon.

Looking back, one of kids' fondest pre-Lizzie memories of Hilary may well be her appearance as the youthful witch Wendy in the 1998 video release of *Casper Meets Wendy*.

The metamorphosis (pardon the pun) of Hilary has been a captivating one indeed: From tutu-twirling ballerina and youthful witch to awkward junior high schooler and handstand walker to teenage pop and movie star—it's truly the stuff dreams are made of!

In the "Kids' Comments" section that follows, we asked kids what they know about Hilary, what they think she might do in the future, and what *they* want to do in the future. As one fan puts it, "Go for your goal!"

KIDS' COMMENTS:

Laura, 10

Radio Disney has had insider stuff about Hilary and her sister where they do interviews with them on the radio, so I've learned a lot about Hilary that way. I listen to Radio Disney all the time, everywhere!

I like Hilary's music. Her acting and music are both really good. I like that you can see both in the movie.

To be like Lizzie would be hard because her brother, Matt, is really annoying—he's like my brother and sister put together. He blackmails Lizzie and would be hard to live with.

But to be like Hilary would be fun and hard. I heard in an interview that it's hard because you have to write songs, make sure your voice has the right tuning, and you have to be ready to go on stage.

I used to take dance and performed on a stage. Then for the Girl Scouts I once got to sing in a talent show. I was kind of nervous, but it was funny at the same time because we all messed up. It was embarrassing but fun because we were performing in front of all our friends, and you're nervous because you don't know if they will like you or hate you.

When I grow up I want to be a professional singer like Hilary. I did a solo in a school play once, but I've never really given much thought to acting. My best friend wants to be an actor though, and I have other friends, so we all kind of want to do it together. It won't hurt to try!

Katharine, 10

I relate to the way Hilary portrays Lizzie's silliness—sometimes she's serious and other times she's silly like me. I like being silly like her. Besides that, I don't know yet what I want to do in the future.

Tess, 9

I think it would be easy to be Hilary because mostly everything is done for you. I want to be an actor in the movies and sing like Hilary. I also want to be an Olympic athlete in skiing, swimming, gymnastics, and soccer. I do all of these sports—and enjoy them all!

Olivia, 11

I like Hilary's music. I've heard it on Radio Disney. I think it would be hard to be Hilary because you have long hours and do a lot of stuff. I think she'll become more of a singer as she gets older. As for me, I want to be a lawyer or a doctor. Hilary has taught me to go for your goal—she stands up to people. I admire that.

Maddie, 11

I know Hilary has a sister who's in one of her TV episodes. It's hard to be Hilary because all her friends are probably jealous.

In the future, I think Hilary might do a mix of TV shows, movies, and singing.

In my future, I want to do stuff in microbiology. My older cousin goes to graduate school for it, and it sounds really fun.

Brigid, 12

I think Hilary will do more shows, plus she may get more singing gigs.

As for me, I'd like to be an author one day. I would also like to be an FBI agent. And I hope before I graduate from high school that I can be on the *American Idol* TV show. I'd probably write some music. I've never written actual notes, but I play the flute and a cool electric keyboard, so I could write the words and sing along with the keyboard.

Michael, 9

Maybe there will be more episodes that show Hilary getting older and older, and when she grows up she'll be in scary movies and stuff.

When I grow up I want to be a professional soccer player.

✻   ✻   ✻

While the media has reported that Hilary plans to pursue other interests apart from her Disney endeavors (such as further Lizzie McGuire *TV episodes and movies), Hilary may very well go on to act film parts that show her growing up. And since her own personal character is linked to that of Lizzie's in many ways, fans may not miss a beat!*

Morgan, 11

It's probably hard to be Hilary Duff because she can't go to regular schools like we do—too many people would crowd around wanting her autograph, and she probably wouldn't like that.

Katelyn, 8

I think it would be really hard to be a star like Hilary because you have lots to do—more than I have.

When I grow up I want to teach kindergarten. I like kids—especially young kids.

Elise, 12

I read in a kids' reader at school that Hilary gets home-schooled, which could get boring because you aren't with people you can relate to. I think it would be hard to be Hilary because you would have to memorize a lot of lines and wouldn't get to hang with your friends as much anymore.

I like Hilary's music. It's not like Britney Spears or Backstreet Boys; I can relate to it better. I think (hope?) she'll be doing a lot more singing in the future.

My future? I want to go into the Air Force because both my grandfathers did. I went to an air and space museum once and took a hands-on flight test and did real well on it. Or I'd like to go into teaching because I like helping young people.

Nicole D., 11

I think the life of a star would be a definite crazy one. You would have to travel all around the world to shoot scenes, and you would probably never get a minute's rest. I think it would be kind of difficult being a star.

I think Hilary has a really good voice, so she might keep going in the actress direction or she might become a singer.

What I'm going to do in the future is be a professional snowboarder.

Curtis, 11

I know about Hilary Duff from watching *Agent Cody Banks*. I think being a star would be awesome, with all those luxuries like limos, private jets, five-star restaurants, and just being famous. I think it can be a little difficult because of all those fans who try so hard to get your autograph and having to wake up early and memorize your lines. I think Hilary will grow up to be a great actress because she already is a tremendous actress. In the future, I would like to play professional lacrosse or be a stuntman.

Kendall, 11

Hilary Duff probably doesn't have the easiest job like some people think. I think Hilary has a really difficult job of being a star. I mean, think of being called a "star" all your life. It must be hard to be a "star" twenty-four hours a day, 7 days a week, 365 days a year. I think Hilary will be a motion picture actress in the future. When I'm older, I want to be either a singer, actress, or teacher.

Nicole K., 10

Hilary Duff as Lizzie McGuire is a good actress because I've seen her TV show and *The Lizzie McGuire Movie,* which seem so realistic in some ways.

I think being a star would be cool because you get room service and everybody would like you and you would be rich!

I think it would be difficult at times because you would have a lot of lines to memorize and you would be asked a lot of questions, too.

I think in the future Hilary will go on to more challenging things and probably have a second movie coming up with exciting adventures.

I don't think I'll be an actress or anything like that, but

what I really would like to do is sports because sports are exciting.

Allie, 11

I watch Hilary's TV show most of the time, and I really enjoy it.

I think being Hilary would be difficult and easy: easy because you don't really have to worry about money and you have somebody to do stuff for you; but difficult because you have to memorize lines and remember all this stuff and always have to be on time.

I want to become an actress, too. I am really interested in theater.

Wendy, 10

I think being a star would be fun because you would probably have a big house, your own cook, maybe even your own hairdresser.

Being a star would be hard though because you would have to memorize all of your lines, and you couldn't go anywhere without people surrounding you asking for your autograph.

I think Hilary will grow into more serious and major acting.

I would like to grow up with Hilary Duff as a role model. She would be a good role model because she always has a good attitude toward everything she does.

Lindsey, 11

I think it would be difficult to be Hilary because when you're out in public, people would come up to you and ask for autographs every day. You might also never get to spend time with your family.

I think Hilary will probably be a singer in the future. In the future, I would want to be a veterinarian.

Jessica, 11

I watch Hilary's show all the time, and I want to see the movie. I think it would be really fun and exciting to be a star, but it would also be very difficult.

I think Hilary will be a famous actress in the future.

When I grow up I want to be a veterinarian or a pro soccer player.

Rhys, 11

It's not easy being a star because you have to study all those lines and deal with the media.

In the future, I'd like to maybe make movies or design sports cars.

Shawn, 11

I think Hilary Duff is a great actress. I know about her because my sister watches her on TV. I think she will become a major star. I want to become an NFL player and make big bucks and own everything!

Savannah, 11

I know that Hilary cares about her friends. Being a star though would get very difficult and stressful because you have to do all kinds of stuff that sometimes you don't want to do.

I think in the future Hilary will go off to college and Kate will be her room buddy. Then they will become best friends, and Gordo and Miranda will have new best friends. Then they will all meet up after a while, and they will be happy to see each other and think back on all their memories.

Cara, 13

I think it's fun to be an actress but also hard because you have so many fans.

I think Hilary will be in many different movies. In the future I want to help animals by being a veterinarian.

Culver, 11

Hilary Duff is a nice, good-looking actress! I think Hilary will be a mom and a good actress (like she already is). I want to be the greatest lacrosse player in the future!

Lacey, 11

I think it is difficult being a star because you always have people asking you for autographs.

I don't know what I want to do in the future, but I think that it would be fun to be in a Disney Channel series.

HiLARY DUFF TiME LiNE

1987: Born September 28

1993: Starts dancing on tour with the Columbus Ballet Met; soon after picks up first acting stint in series of TV commercials

1997: Acts in TV miniseries, *True Women*

1998: Plays Wendy in *Casper Meets Wendy*

1999: Plays Ellie in made-for-TV movie, *The Soul Collector;* won Young Artist Award for Best Supporting Young Actress

2001: Stars in *Lizzie McGuire* TV sit-com

2002: Acts in *Cadet Kelly* original movie on the Disney Channel

2003, Spring: Release of movie sound track including the catchy "Why Not" and "What Dreams Are Made Of." Also includes punchy song, "Girl in the Band," by Hil's big sister, Haylie. Also films *Cheaper by the Dozen* and begins prefilming for movie *The Cinderella Story*

2003, Late Summer: Release of first solo album, *Metamorphosis*

2003, Fall: *Lizzie McGuire* TV show enters second season

Your imaginary Friend

(On the Real Hil)

Lights, camera, action! Oh, to be a star! Just imagine: All those bright lights might make your drab, old regular life fade into the shadows . . . to be replaced by limos, admiring fans, and even your own makeup and clothing line. . . .

OK, back to reality. Life as a famous actor or singer isn't all fantasy and fanfare. You've still got to study hard in school, for example. (Hilary homeschools, spending hours with her tutor each day, on top of singing lessons and hours spent doing and redoing film scenes . . . *and* she wants to go to college one day!) And imagine if you have a bad hair day—then what? You've got to face the raving crowds, messy hair and all!

It could be worth the "crazy chance" to pursue a life of glamour, but just remember that getting there requires a lot of hard work. And even once you're *there,* you may find that your favorite thing to do—like Hilary—is to just "hang with friends."

No matter where you are or go in life, friends make all the difference!

9

Some of Our Favorite Scenes

KiDS' COMMENTS:

Bailey, 11

I liked the parts in the movie with the teacher, Ms. Unger-meyer, who was Lizzie's chaperone in Rome. She's not your average teacher: She's strong and can defend herself.

Karyssa, 12

I love the episode when Lizzie and Gordo disguise Larry so that he can go to Miranda's party, and when Miranda finds out first she screams but then she realizes that she should have invited him in the first place. I like this for two reasons: first, because they learn to accept Larry, and second, because it was funny how they dressed him up to look cool.

Michael, 9

I watch Lizzie on TV every day. I like how good Gordo is at playing hacky sack and Matt is good at doing pranks on his sister and Sam [Lizzie's dad] is obsessed with football.

Katilyn, 13

My favorite scene is when Lizzie is in her room and she starts to sing because I like to sing but not in front of anyone.

Courtney, 12

I think every Lizzie episode is fab. I really liked the episode when Lizzie and Miranda made a music video.

❊   ❊   ❊

Courtney is referring to the TV episode when Lizzie and Miranda decide to make a music video for a school project and put Gordo in charge of filming it. When Miranda sees herself on film the following day, she unrealistically sees an oversized version of herself and immediately decides to go on a crash diet. (As many people know, cameras can "add" several pounds to your image.)

When Miranda eventually passes out from sheer hunger, her pals try to get her to talk. "Talking to your friends can help," they insist. And they're right: Miranda realizes how silly her starva-

tion plan really was and admits that she was trying to control her life—which at times felt out of control—by not eating.

In the end, the trio produces a fabulous music video after all. That's what friends are for!

Maddie, 11

I like both the TV show and the movie—they're so true to life, the way reality shows are, and the characters are funny. My little sister likes it a lot, too.

Ashley, 11

My favorite scene with Lizzie in the movie is when she meets Paolo because it's weird.

*   *   *

When Lizzie meets Paolo in the movie, it is indeed "weird" and almost dreamlike: Tossing a coin in the Trevi Fountain results in the European pop star's appearance—and an opportunity for Lizzie to pursue "a chance to do anything I wanna do." Have you ever tossed a coin in a fountain and made a wish? Just think: Your dreams may come true—even if it's in a totally weird way!

Annabel, 8

I love watching the different episodes every weekend on TV, and I've seen the movie two times!

I like the way Lizzie and her brother, Matt, always interact with each other, calling each other funny names. In one episode, for example, where Lizzie wanted to get tickets to a Christmas show with guest star Aaron Carter, Matt made a deal with Lizzie to show her the place where the show was being performed. (Later, Lizzie got to sing and dance with Aaron; I used to like him!) In another episode, Matt and his friend went undercover to try to fix something that Kate messed up, while Lizzie was the disc jockey at a school dance. It was funny the way they talked to each other!

Amanda, 10

I like the episode where a statue gets broken in the school courtyard and then Lizzie tries to fix it with bubblegum. It was funny because I've never seen anyone try to fix something that way—usually you'd try to fix something like that with cement!

❧ ❧ ❧

As a "huge" fan of Lizzie's and a frequent reader of other books about the young starlet, Amanda gets the award for actually coming up with the idea for this book! "I thought a book that told more about Lizzie would be a good idea," says the young potential editor. Go, girl!

Merissa, 10

I like the part in the movie when Lizzie is modeling her outfits and all of them do something that is not good!

❧ ❧ ❧

In her attempt to mimic diva pop star Isabella in The Lizzie McGuire Movie, *Lizzie allows herself to be subjected to a barrage of wild, outlandish outfits imposed upon her by an intimidating, snooty costume crew. While one might think the opportunity to try on a series of top fashion outfits would be the stuff dreams are made of, Lizzie soon appears exhausted and defeated by so many trials. What looks best, it turns out, is Lizzie's own simple yet somehow highly stylish getup. Sometimes what's hidden in the back of your own closet is better than all the diva gowns in the world!*

Katharine, 10

I started to like Lizzie after watching a Lizzie McGuire marathon on TV. That's where they show lots of episodes one right after the other. The situations on the show sometimes teach you how to solve problems. All the characters do funny things, and the cartoon Lizzie adds spark to it.

Tess, 9

I went to see the movie two times, and I loved the graduation scene best because it was funny; and after Lizzie's brother videotaped it, it was on *Good Morning America!* I can relate to Lizzie because my little brother tells his friends about funny stuff I do, too.

Nicole P., 10

My favorite part of the movie was when she was singing on stage because she looks like a real singer.

❖   ❖   ❖

As most readers know by now, Lizzie (or at least the actress who portrays her, Hilary Duff) IS a real singer—and an up-and-coming one at that!

Cody, 12

My favorite scene is when Lizzie tries to be like Angel.

Devin, 7

My favorite scene is when Ethan takes his test after Lizzie tutored him.

❀ ❀ ❀

Ethan Craft isn't known for his smarts but rather for his general good looks and long, glossy hair. When his participation in sports is put in jeopardy due to flunking a class, sensible Gordo tries to come to the rescue. But even Gordo's efforts are lost on the athlete. Then when Lizzie tries to help Ethan, she finds she has a knack for explaining math in terms of counting hair accessories. Like, duh! What better way to explain something to the "hottie"? Ethan ends up getting a "B" on his test—a record for the below-average student. Could Lizzie and Ethan be a match made in heaven?

Melinda, 12

I like the scene when Lizzie and Gordo are in the library right after she breaks up with Ronny because Gordo says really sweet things.

❀ ❀ ❀

Lizzie first gets to know Ronny as the boy from a different school who delivers her family's newspaper. Lizzie develops a crush on Ronny, driving her regular pals crazy with her pining away for him. And funnily enough, Gordo expresses jealousy in one scene where Ronny kisses Lizzie! It turns out Gordo only had Lizzie's best interests in mind; however, when Ronny ends up dumping Lizzie for someone else, leaving Lizzie crushed, Gordo comes quickly to the rescue with the reassuring words only a good pal can provide.

Morgen, 11

My favorite scene is when Lizzie is giving advice to people on the computer.

Elise, 12

There is an episode where Miranda has a big party and invites everyone except Larry because she thinks he's a queer person. I liked how Lizzie helped Larry become someone else because when he changed, Miranda liked him better than before.

Heather, 10

I liked how in the movie Gordo took the blame from Ms. Ungermeyer for sneaking out at night so Lizzie wouldn't get in trouble for sneaking out with Paolo. I like it because he did it because of the love in his heart for Lizzie.

❧   ❧   ❧

Gordo covers for Lizzie in the movie even though she ditched him for an adventure with the more romantic Paolo. As her good friend,

he knows how important it was for her to take a "crazy chance"—
even if it meant leaving him behind for a while.

Annie, 8

I think it's a really kid-friendly show, and I see Lizzie as a
role model for how I'd like to be when I'm older. Lizzie
takes a lot of risks that she makes look easy. Like, in one TV
episode she showed Kate how to do a one-handed stunt in
her gym class. I know how to do a two-handed handstand,
but not a one-handed one. And Lizzie's pretty, too. She has
a really nice smile and teeth. I'd like to be an actress like
her one day, too.

Your imaginary Friend

(On Favorite Scenes)

"I just love Lizzie!" rave the show's fans. Have you ever
stopped to wonder why? You and your pals wish more than
anything that you could be like Lizzie, and even your
younger brothers and sisters have been known to sit—
chuckling regularly—through an entire episode featuring a
day in the life of the junior high schooler (imagining—
what—how to be as perfectly pesky as Lizzie's little brother,
Matt? Scary!).

One way the show keeps kids on the edge of their seats
is through fun, light, humor-rendering techniques, including background sound effects (bleeps, boings, blinks,
squeaks, and highlights of theme songs to highlight characters' feelings or expressions) as well as exaggerated flash-

backs or imaginary "what-if-type" scenarios experienced by Lizzie and her family and friends. (And what kid doesn't like exaggerating?) It's a whole lot more creative and effective than, say, the canned applause or laughter you might see in some older TV sit-coms. What's more, the show seems real without taking on the qualities of some gruesome reality show. We see how much Lizzie's parents and friends really care for her, but we *don't* see people calling each other really mean names or putting each other down (except for the periodic expressions of normal frustration with a pesky little brother, for example . . . and who can blame a kid for that?).

At the end of each episode, everything seems to come out OK, which ideally we'd all like to see in our own lives—especially if we can do so while keeping a smile on our faces!

10 ✳

Speaking of Which...

Test your knowledge of your tween vernacular know-how here with our list compiled from tween contributors across the country. Perhaps you have some terms of your own to add, or you could act as editor and update our list—as many of the terms go out of style faster than you can say, "Like, no way!"

✿ ✿ ✿

"Awesome"
What it means: "Very cool"
Explanation: When kids use it, the word takes on a lighter meaning than when adults use it in its more conventional way. A sparkly new fashion accessory can be "awesome," for example, but not to the extent that it actually commands

jaw-dropping *awe*. Taking a trip to Rome was much more awesome for Lizzie and her pals in *The Lizzie McGuire Movie* than the less exciting alternative: going to "Waterslide Wonderland's."

❧ ❧ ❧

"BF"
What it means: "Best friend"
Explanation: The acronym is one of many to probably get its start in the casually written world of E-mail. Lizzie's BF? Miranda and Gordo share that honor.

❧ ❧ ❧

"Coolness"
What it means: "That's cool"
Explanation: Yet another way to affirm that something is indeed cool. If a guy says he got a new skateboard, his buddy might reply, "Coolness." Ethan Craft is known to use the word to describe just about anything that's above average.

❧ ❧ ❧

"Dissed"
What it means: "Shown disrespect"
Explanation: Your pal "disses" you if she talks about you behind your back. The word made its debut in the world of rap music and has since gone mainstream.

※ ※ ※

"Ditched"
What it means: "Left stranded"
Explanation: If you left your friend at the library without telling her you were leaving, she'd say you "ditched" her. Lizzie and her pals frequently struggle with feeling ditched by one friend or another.

※ ※ ※

"Dude"
What it means: "Guy"
Explanation: "Dude" is used as a noun to refer to a person; it also sometimes means, "Hey, you." "Dudes," Ethan Craft might say casually upon meeting up with some buddies.

※ ※ ※

"Fab"
What it means: "Fabulous"
Explanation: A cousin of "fave," the shortened term "fab" has a rather sophisticated ring to it, even when used by a junior high schooler like Lizzie.

※ ※ ※

"Fam"
What it means: "Family"

Explanation: Like its cousins, "bro" or "sis," it only makes sense to shorten "family" to "fam."

❀   ❀   ❀

"Fan"
What it means: "Fantastic"
Explanation: Lizzie did a "fan" job singing at the Colosseum in Rome.

❀   ❀   ❀

"Fave"
What it means: "Favorite"
Explanation: "Fave" is naturally more smooth sounding than if you enunciate the entire word with all those excess vowel sounds!

❀   ❀   ❀

"Fine"
What it means: "Looking good"
Explanation: If someone calls you "fine," you know you're looking your best!

❀   ❀   ❀

"Fink"
What it means: "Tattletale"
Explanation: Lizzie raises her eyebrows when Gordo sug-

gests people might think she's a "fink." "You know, rat, stool pigeon, snitch," he explains.

✿ ✿ ✿

"Flip side"
What it means: "Tomorrow"
Explanation: See ya on the "flip side!"

✿ ✿ ✿

"Fruit"
What it means: "Someone who does something hilarious" or "an annoying person"
Explanation: See "fruitcake" explanation below. The words seem to be fairly interchangeable, as well as have, in some cases, opposite meanings!

✿ ✿ ✿

"Fruitcake"
What it means: "Funny person"
Explanation: Her friend was always being silly, so they called her a "fruitcake."

✿ ✿ ✿

"Gotta motor"
What it means: "I need to go now"
Explanation: If it's time to split from a party or gym practice,

you might say, "Gotta motor." Of course, in the case of junior high schoolers like Lizzie and pals, it doesn't mean *literally* motor, as they're still waiting to get their drivers' licenses!

❄   ❄   ❄

"I like"
What it means: "I like something"
Explanation: Many tweens enjoy shortening the phrase and quipping, "I like" rather than "I like it."

❄   ❄   ❄

"Mathlete"
What it means: A cross between "math geek" and athlete—someone who can't get anything right
Explanation: Lizzie's worst fear in one TV episode, where she's in charge of decorations for a school dance, is that she'll mess up and be considered a "mathlete" by her peers.

❄   ❄   ❄

"Peeps"
What it means: "Your close pals"
Explanation: Take a word like "people," cut off the end of it and add an "s," and you've got a fun word for your best buddies. Gordo and Miranda are Lizzie's "peeps."

❀ ❀ ❀

"Reeks"
What it means: "Terrible"
Explanation: That test really "reeks." (Also another word for a similar slang word, "stinks.")

❀ ❀ ❀

"Right"
What it means: "Whatever"
Explanation: Said with just the right amount of blaséness, saying "Right" is a good way to let something you don't agree with roll past you.

❀ ❀ ❀

"Score"
What it means: "All right"
Explanation: If you got a candy bar with your lunch, you might say, "Score!"

❀ ❀ ❀

"See ya later, alligator!"
What it means: "Good-bye"
Explanation: There are so many cute ways to say good-bye or, as Lizzie puts it in her movie, "Ciao!" the Italian way of saying good-bye, pronounced, "chow."

❀ ❀ ❀

"Sevie"
What it means: "Seventh grader"
Explanation: The sixth graders were looking forward to being "sevies" after graduating. (Note: Some kids have been known to say "sevenny" instead.)

❀ ❀ ❀

"Sick"
What it means: "Cool"
Explanation: "A lot of boys say this to mean the opposite of what its regular meaning is," reports one eleven-year-old girl from California. Young kids seem to enjoy experimenting with "opposite" word games this way—like their own version of secret pig latin.

❀ ❀ ❀

"Sweet"
What it means: "That's nice"
Explanation: If a kid got an "A" on a test, his buddy might say, "Sweet."

❀ ❀ ❀

"Tight"
What it means: "Cool"

Explanation: The options seem endless: Here's yet another way to express how cool something is!

✣ ✣ ✣

"Total hottie"
What it means: "Very cute guy/girl"
Explanation: Lizzie is so enamored with Ethan in one episode that she refers to him as "A total hottie." (Synonyms include "hunk" and "heartthrob.")

✣ ✣ ✣

"Totally"
What it means: "Yes"
Explanation: If you liked a party, you might say, "Totally."

✣ ✣ ✣

"Totally raw"
What it means: "Very cool"
Explanation: Gordo makes a "totally raw" slam dunk into the basketball hoop at gym practice.

✣ ✣ ✣

"Way freaky"
What it means: "Very weird"
Explanation: Something that is just slightly out of the norm

can be a very scary experience for a highly sensitive, self-conscious tween like Lizzie. In the *Lizzie McGuire* TV show, viewers can usually tell something's "way freaky" when they hear the background screeching sound effects made famous by the old *Psycho* movie.

❧   ❧   ❧

"Whatever"
What it means: "I couldn't care less"
Explanation: When pronounced with singsongy Valley Girl emphasis on the middle syllable, the phrase has a snobby, dismissive appeal. (Kate is famous for saying this!)

❧   ❧   ❧

"Wicked"
What it means: "Awesome" or "really cool"
Explanation: Lizzie bought some "wicked" new hip huggers at the mall.

❧   ❧   ❧

"W'sup?"
What it means: "How are you doing?"
Explanation: This casual greeting undoubtedly rolls off the tongue more easily than the traditional greeting.

❧   ❧   ❧

"Yo"

What it means: "Hey"

Explanation: Saying "Yo" can be a good way to get someone's attention before you talk to them. Like, "Yo, Lizzie!"

And the Award Goes to . . .

Read all the young people's responses to Lizzie McGuire throughout this book, and you might notice some common threads: That is, while every respondent has a very unique perspective (just as you and your friends have different hair colors, eye colors, and other features), there are some details that seem to pop up again and again (just as you and your friends might buy the same shoes or say the same phrases). There is, indeed, a pattern of *likenesses* that emerges from the outlook of tweens just about everywhere.

With that in mind, we've come up with our own sort of awards ceremony. Drum roll, please! And the award goes to . . .

✿   ✿   ✿

Favorite Stylish Outfit of Lizzie's: Her Roman concert attire in the movie.

❋ ❋ ❋

Favorite Everyday Outfit of Lizzie's: Jeans and T-shirt (don't let the plainness of this description fool you though; those are most likely sequined or specially washed, low-slung jeans and a delicately decorated T).

❋ ❋ ❋

Most Common Tween Saying: "Sweet."

❋ ❋ ❋

Funniest Scene: A tie between falling into a trash can and falling on the stage at graduation.

❋ ❋ ❋

Best Way to Handle Bullies: Ignore 'em.

❋ ❋ ❋

Consensus on Hilary's Career: Long hours, tough demands.

❋ ❋ ❋

Consensus on Hilary's Future: More acting and definitely more singing.

✿ ✿ ✿

How Parents Drive You Crazy: Tell you to clean this or that.

✿ ✿ ✿

Kid's Favorite Dream Future: Singer, teacher, or veterinarian.

✿ ✿ ✿

Best Way to Stay Friends: Stick together.

Resources

Chocolate for a Teen's Spirit: Simon & Schuster, 2002. Author Kay Allenbaugh compiles stories for young women "about hope, strength, and wisdom." Geared more toward teens than tweens; however, it's still a good source of stories on setting goals, rising above difficult times, and nurturing faith in yourself.

http://kidshealth.org: This Web site includes helpful sections on dealing with feelings from peer pressure and gossip to bullies, cheating, and special needs.

Private and Personal: Questions and Answers for Girls Only: HarperCollins, 2000. A compilation of advice about school, friends, family, and more for tweens and teens alike by Carol Weston, the advice columnist from *Girls' Life Magazine.*

Check your local library in the junior readers' section for a copy of the handbook.

www.americangirl.com: A Web site based on the magazine *American Girl* (available by mail subscription or in many libraries on the magazine rack in the junior readers' section) that explores many of the issues girls face today.

www.disney.go.com: Home of the Disney Channel online. Lizzie news, quizzes, activities, photos, and style tips.

www.disneystore.com: Source for purchasing Disney's Lizzie-related items, including sound tracks and books.

www.girlslife.com: Based on *Girls' Life Magazine* (available by mail subscription or in many libraries on the magazine rack in the junior readers' section). A resource for girls ages ten to fifteen, includes advice on friends, family, school, crushes, fashion, and beauty.

www.hilaryduff.com: The official Hilary Duff fan site, includes Hilary's own regularly updated diary, pictures, a biography, news, and dates for Hilary's upcoming events and tours, and "ask Hilary" E-mail opportunities with an archive of Hilary's past responses.

About the Author

Guen Sublette is a writer and editor in the foothills outside Denver, Colorado, where she balances being mom to two pre-tweens with writing about children's and family issues for various publications. She is also the author of the popular reference trade paperback *The Book of Days* (Berkley Group).